THE
GHOSTLY TALES
OF
DALLAS

T0019712

For Old Bill Edwards, my favorite ghost

Published by Arcadia Children's Books
A Division of Arcadia Publishing
Charleston, SC
www.arcadiapublishing.com

Spooky America is a trademark of Arcadia Publishing, Inc.

First published 2023

Manufactured in the United States

ISBN 978-1-4671-9727-4

Library of Congress Control Number: 2023931844

All images used courtesy of Shutterstock.com; p. 2 jmanaugh3/Shutterstock.com; p. 8 Gilberto Mesquita/Shutterstock.com; p. 18 Kit Leong/Shutterstock.com; p. 23 4kclips/Shutterstock.com; p. 24 Kelleher Photography/Shutterstock.com.

Notice: The information in this book is true and complete to the best of our knowledge. It is offered without guarantee on the part of the author or Arcadia Publishing. The author and Arcadia Publishing disclaim all liability in connection with the use of this book.

Spooky America

THE
GHOSTLY TALES
OF

DALLAS

CARIE JUETTNER

Adapted from *Haunted Dallas* by Rita Cook

arcadia
CHILDREN'S BOOKS

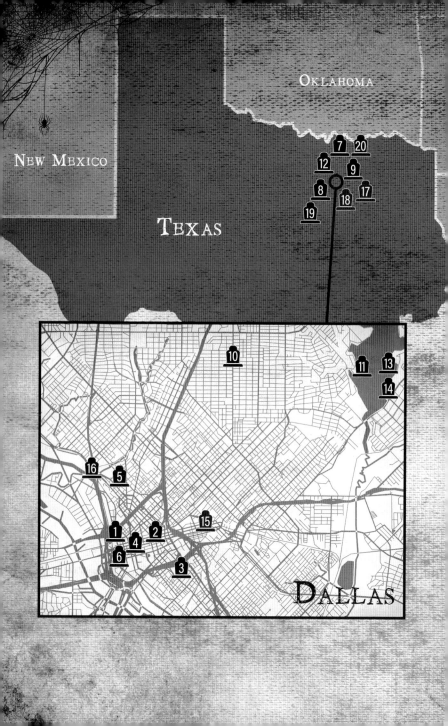

TABLE OF CONTENTS & MAP KEY

Welcome to Spooky Dallas! 3

Chapter 1. Downtown Disturbances 9
1. Texas School Book Depository
2. Majestic Theater

3. Chapter 2. Old Souls in Old City Park 19

Chapter 3. Haunted Hotels and Cemeteries 25
4. The Adolphus Hotel
5. The Stoneleigh Hotel
6. Hotel Lawrence
7. Baccus Cemetery
8. Pleasant Valley Cemetery
9. Mills Cematary

10. Chapter 4. Strange Sights at Snuffer's 39

11. Chapter 5. The Lady of White Rock Lake 43

12. Chapter 6. Unexpected Experiences at Unity of Dallas 55

Chapter 7. Ghosts with Good Taste 59
13. The Dallas Arboretum and Botanical Garden
14. DeGolyer House
15. Sons of Hermann Hall
16. Sammons Center for the Arts

Chapter 8. Spooky Suburbs 71
17. Red Oak
18. Waxahachie
19. Cleburne

20. Chapter 9. Mysteries in McKinney 91

A Ghostly Goodbye 105

The red pegasus in Dallas

Welcome to Spooky Dallas!

Home of the Dallas Cowboys football team, the famous Flying Red Horse landmark, and the tragic location of President John F. Kennedy's assassination, Dallas, Texas, is a city known far and wide for its history, skyscrapers, and opportunities for fun. But did you know it's also a destination for ghost sightings?

The thriving metropolis that Dallasites know today began as a small settlement on the

Trinity River. John Neely Bryan founded Dallas in 1841. At the end of 1849, 163 people lived there. By 2021, the population had grown to almost 1.3 million.

At first, the young city attracted people because it proved to be a good location for growing crops. Soon, people in other professions began settling there, such as doctors, lawyers, and educators. The arrival of the railroad and the telegraph in the 1870s

brought even more business to the area. Dallas was already well on its way to becoming the booming city it is today. But based on some of the spooky sensations people get when visiting historic sites, it seems that some of Dallas's early settlers may have stuck around . . . *permanently.*

Quite a few famous names have been connected with Dallas over the years, including some well-known outlaws. Some of the most recognizable names connected with Dallas don't belong to real people. J.R. and Sue Ellen Ewing were the main characters on a TV show called *Dallas* that ran from 1978 to 1991. Tourists still tour Southfork Ranch where the show was filmed.

These days, people come to Dallas for the shopping, art, and, of course, fried foods. The State Fair of Texas, held annually in Dallas's Fair Park, is famous for its unique dining choices. Over the years, visitors have enjoyed fried Coca-Cola, fried peanut butter and jelly sandwiches, and even fried fruit salad! But if you take a trek to see Big Tex, the fair's fifty-foot-tall, cowboy-hatted and boot-wearing mascot, the cuisines you consume might not be the *only* weird things you encounter during your stay. Spirits haunt several of Dallas's popular hotels and restaurants. Linger long enough, and you're bound to run into one.

But don't expect to escape eerie experiences by avoiding the haunted buildings. Dallas's most well-known specter, the Lady of White Rock Lake, haunts one of the city's most popular outdoor spots.

As you can see, ghosts are alive and well (metaphorically speaking) deep in the heart of Texas. Read on to meet some of them!

The Majestic Theater, Dallas

Downtown Disturbances

Downtown Dallas is a lively area humming with activity. The central business district is known for its upscale shopping, museums, and many eateries, including the famous revolving restaurant at the top of Reunion Tower. Dallas's downtown appeals to tourists and residents alike, but not all the attractions are happy ones. Tragedy and terror await in some of the downtown buildings.

On November 22, 1963, Dallas became famous worldwide for a shocking and terrible event: President John F. Kennedy's assassination. JFK was the country's youngest president, and he was beloved by many. On that fateful day in November 1963, he and his wife, Jackie, were visiting Dallas. They were riding past Dealey Plaza in a convertible limo with the top down when shots rang out, killing the president and wounding John Connelly, the Texas governor. The president was only forty-six years old when he died. His murder shocked the world and stamped the city of Dallas with tragedy forevermore.

Mystery and controversy still surround the details of the president's assassination, but Lee Harvey Oswald was charged with the murder. Officials say he fired the rifle shots from a window on the sixth floor of the Texas School Book Depository at the corner of Houston and

Elm. Oswald never made it to trial, though. Two days after his arrest, while being transported to a different jail, he was also murdered by a man named Jack Ruby.

The red brick Texas School Book Depository was built in 1901. At the time of JFK's assassination, the building stocked and distributed textbooks to public schools in north Texas and Oklahoma. In 1977, the City of Dallas acquired the building and renovated it, leaving the top two floors (including the space where Oswald fired the fatal shots) empty. However, in 1989, the famous floor reopened as the Sixth Floor Museum, a place where people can learn about the president's assassination and its impact on the nation.

With so much sadness and death associated with the area, it's no wonder many say the Sixth Floor Museum is haunted. Several people have reported seeing a shadowy figure wandering the halls of the exhibit. They see it out of the corner of their eyes, but when they turn to look directly at the shape, it vanishes. Unexplained cold spots also exist, and photos and videos taken there often end up revealing orbs or mists unseen by the naked eye. Sometimes people outside the building look up at the infamous sixth-floor window, where Oswald waited for JFK's motorcade to come by, and see an eerie figure looking down at them.

The Sixth Floor Museum is a somber memorial of a terrible moment in the country's history. You may well feel the sadness that surrounds this event, and you are not alone. The whole world mourned the loss of President John F. Kennedy, and the shadows, mists, and orbs present in the building on Elm Street suggest some spirits remain there, mourning him still.

Another haunted but less melancholy structure in downtown Dallas is the aptly named Majestic Theater. Just a few blocks down Elm Street from the Sixth Floor Museum stands the beautiful Renaissance Revival-style building with its ornate windows and iconic neon sign proclaiming "The Majestic." The theater's magnificence continues inside with Corinthian columns, grand staircases, marble floors, and a fan-shaped auditorium. Karl Hoblitzelle opened the theater in 1921, and it recently celebrated its hundredth anniversary.

The first shows to take the stage at the Majestic were vaudeville acts, a type of

entertainment popular in the early 1900s. The theater enjoyed success for decades, but after Hoblitzelle died in 1967, the Majestic's business began to decline until it closed its doors in 1973. However, the building was donated to the City of Dallas in 1976. After a major renovation, it reopened in 1983 and is still delighting audiences today with shows and musicals. Though much has changed over the years about the type of performances the theater presents, the majesty it was named for remains, and people come from all around to enjoy its entertainment, beauty, and history.

Something else—or *someone* else—remains at the Majestic, too. Some people think the theater's beloved original owner may still be hanging around as a spirit. Telephone lines light up on their own, and backdrops have been known to lower without any (living) human moving them. Employees sometimes smell food cooking when no one is in the kitchen, and more than one person has reported hearing disembodied voices floating through the building. The spirit itself can even be felt at times. Random cold spots appear in the theater, and some have experienced the

sensation of being touched when no other person is visible.

Why do people think Karl Hoblitzelle is the spirit of the Majestic? Well, no one could blame the owner for wanting to stick around his pride and joy. He must be thrilled the theater is still open and successful more than a hundred years after he built it. Plus, much of the ghostly activity occurs on the fifth floor of the building, and that's exactly where Hoblitzelle's portrait hung for many years. Some used to find the image disturbing, saying that something behind the painted eyes seemed to look back at them.

The portrait no longer hangs at the Majestic, and reports of hauntings have decreased in recent years, so Karl Hoblitzelle may have retired from the theater industry for good. But there are still plenty of reasons to take a trip to Dallas's oldest theater. You can bask in its beauty, enjoy a show, and *maybe* even experience a ghostly brush with the past while you're there.

Blum Bros. General Store building in Old City Park

Old Souls in Old City Park

Sometimes it can be difficult to picture a place as it used to be. When looking at Dallas today—with its seventy-story skyscrapers and six-lane highways—it's hard to imagine the city as it was in the 1800s. Fortunately, if you take a trip to Old City Park, you don't have to imagine. It's like stepping back into the past.

The scenic, twenty-acre park is home to almost two dozen buildings from the nineteenth century. These historic homes and businesses have been moved from other locations across Texas to educate people about the past and allow them to enjoy spending some time in a bygone era. Among its many structures, Old City Park includes a bank, school, general store, blacksmith shop, train depot, hotel, restaurant, law office, and several houses. Each building is furnished accurately for the time period, displaying tools, equipment, and objects used by people in their daily lives. Oh, and a few of the buildings also come with ghosts.

The train depot, which was built in Fate, Texas, in the 1880s, houses a shy ghost. The spirit of an elderly Black man sometimes peers out from behind the storage room door. However, if anyone goes to look for him, he vanishes. Thankfully, this bashful phantom seems harmless. The ghost that resides in the law office may have suffered a violent death. The building once housed a grocery store in east Dallas. A man was murdered by the mob (another word for a secret, organized group of criminals) in that store, and some believe the victim may still be wandering the place where he died.

The most haunted structure in Old City Park, though, is definitely Millermore Mansion. This two-story, white, columned home from the Civil War era is the largest remaining historic mansion in Dallas. When guests step inside, the fireplaces, oil lamps, and authentic Civil War furnishings transport them back in time. Another thing that makes visitors feel like they're in the past is when they see a woman from the 1800s walk by.

Guests, staff, and volunteers at

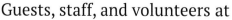

Old City Park have witnessed a female ghost on the second floor. She stands in an upstairs window wearing a light-colored dress in mid-1800s fashion. Unexplainable cold spots appear in the house as well, and sometimes objects are relocated by unseen hands.

Who is the woman who haunts Millermore Mansion? She may be the spirit of the original owner's wife. William Brown Miller began construction on the Millermore Mansion in 1855. His wife, Minerva Barnes Miller, died a year later, before the house was completed. Those who have seen the specter on the second floor say she bears a strong resemblance to Minerva.

If you're interested in Dallas's history, take a trip to Old City Park. Be on the lookout while you're there. You may just run into someone from the past.

Millermore Mansion

The Adolphus Hotel

Haunted Hotels and Cemeteries

Whether it's a home or a hotel, a bunkhouse or a bed-and-breakfast, everyone needs a place to lay their head at night, even ghosts.

Three landmark hotels still decorate the Dallas landscape: The Adolphus Hotel, the Stoneleigh Hotel, and Hotel Lawrence. Rumor has it that a few guests at these historic hotels have overstayed their welcome.

Built in 1912, the Adolphus on Commerce Street is Dallas's oldest hotel and still one of its most luxurious. For several years, the twenty-one-story hotel held the title of the tallest building in Texas. These days, the Adolphus poses no contest to the skyscrapers of Dallas's skyline, but it still stands out as one of the city's most impressive structures. Although the building is over one hundred years old, it hasn't lost its elegance. The Adolphus boasts stylish décor and vintage touches throughout, including a beautifully carved grand piano in the French Room Salon.

The Adolphus Hotel has welcomed many famous visitors over the years, including

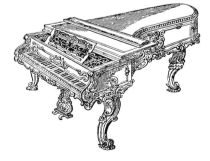

baseball legend Babe Ruth and Queen Elizabeth II. However, it's the ghostly guests who make the biggest impression on people these days.

The sounds of a party—swing music and the noisy chatter of partygoers—have been known to drift up and down the halls of the Adolphus, even when no one is there. Perhaps these are the echoes of the celebrations that used to occur in the ballroom on the nineteenth floor. Renovations in the 1970s altered this area, turning the ballroom into more guest rooms, but maybe the merriment of those earlier years lives on.

Not every ballroom memory was a happy one, though. Long ago, a bride took her own life after being left at the altar in that ballroom. Some people say they can still sense her presence at the hotel.

It feels like a warm current of air enveloping them in sadness.

Then again, not every ghost sticks around due to tragedy. Former hotel employees claim that a regular customer of the Adolphus chose to keep coming back after her death. They'd spot her sitting at her favorite table, enjoying the amenities of the Adolphus even in the afterlife.

The Stoneleigh Hotel, built in 1923, and Hotel Lawrence, built just two years later in 1925, have also endured over the decades of change in Dallas, and both have some spooky stories to tell.

Standing eleven stories tall on Maple Avenue in Dallas's Uptown District, the swanky Stoneleigh Hotel has housed a wide range of celebrities, from actors such as Judy Garland (Dorothy in *The Wizard of Oz*) to popular singers like LeAnn Rimes, who became a country music star at age thirteen. If you stay at this luxury hotel, don't forget to pamper yourself with a spa treatment. The spa is located in the basement, and some say that area of the building is haunted. While getting a manicure or massage to lift your spirits, you may end up *seeing* a spirit!

The Hotel Lawrence, which is now the La Quinta Inn & Suites by Wyndham, also has a few ghosts wandering around. Located near the West End District, this historic structure is still a popular destination for tourists visiting Dallas, but its past may surprise some of its current guests. Rumors suggest the basement of the hotel may have been a hotspot for illegal gambling in the 1920s and 1930s, and the top floor of the ten-story building saw its share of tragedies. A woman staying in room 1009 jumped off the roof in the

1940s, and a congressman later took his own life in room 1015.

These dreadful events could be the cause of the eerie phenomena people have experienced at the hotel. Employees feel watched by unseen eyes when they are in the basement, and some have seen a man dressed in black wandering around down there. Elevators at the hotel have been known to get stuck at 1:30 a.m., and more than one guest has reported hearing an unexpected knock on

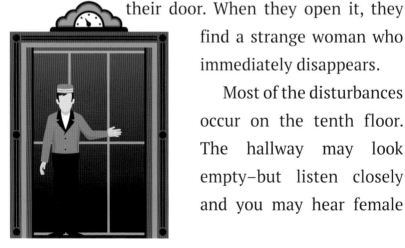

their door. When they open it, they find a strange woman who immediately disappears.

Most of the disturbances occur on the tenth floor. The hallway may look empty—but listen closely and you may hear female voices drifting by; take a picture and it may reveal spooky spheres of light. However, the eighth floor has its own ghost. People call him "Smiley" and say if you talk to him nicely, you can get on his good side. So, if you visit the old Hotel Lawrence, be sure to have a kind word for Smiley. After all, you wouldn't want to be on a ghost's bad side, would you?

While some of Dallas's ghosts obviously prefer the top-notch accommodations of the city's famous hotels, others are happy to hang out in more appropriate locations for the dead, such as cemeteries. Legends, myths, and tales of spooky sensations abound at the cemeteries in and around Dallas.

An imposing iron gate guards the graveyard at the Baccus Cemetery in the Dallas suburb of Plano. Shopping centers and restaurants surround the small space now, but the land goes way back. The Baccus Cemetery started out as the Cook Cemetery in 1847. It includes one of the area's oldest graves: the burial place of Henry Cook, a veteran of the War of 1812. The cemetery changed names in 1915, and the town of Plano grew up around it, but the spirits of those buried there stuck around.

Visitors to this old graveyard experience cold spots that can't be explained and hear voices and footsteps from unidentified sources. Orbs often appear in photographs taken there, and a few people have reported seeing a

shadowy figure crossing the cemetery grounds.

People who grew up near the Pleasant Valley Cemetery in Cedar Hill, south of Dallas, have some strange stories to tell. Pleasant Valley, which earned the nicknames "Witch Mountain," "Ghost Mountain," and "Old Spook Hill" at various times over the years, experienced some unfortunate events in the past. Vandals trashed the cemetery, defacing tombstones and destroying property. People told tales of devil worshippers congregating there on full-moon nights, and there were even some reports of grave robbing. Then stories began to emerge of a "goat man" who prowled the graveyard at night. The legends said he was on the lookout for grave robbers and other wrongdoers.

In 1995, the Pleasant Valley Cemetery was named a Texas historical landmark, and measures were taken to protect it. However, that doesn't mean the goat man doesn't still roam there.

Mills Cemetery in the Dallas suburb of Garland contains a unique grave with a tragic past. A single tombstone marks the burial place of five members of the Smiley family. The grave marker lists the names and birthdates of the mother, father, and three daughters. At the bottom, it reads, "All died May 9, 1927." Rumors and myths prevail about the Smiley family. Some even claim their deaths were the result of a murder/suicide. But the heartbreaking truth is that the Smileys were victims of a violent tornado that tore through Garland in the middle of the night on May 9, 1927. Five

members of the family perished in the storm, while two daughters survived.

The Smiley grave site gives off an overwhelming feeling of sadness to many who visit. Some say if you lie down on the grave on Halloween, you will have trouble getting back up.

Though there's no guarantee you'll experience the otherworldly if you visit one of these places, you might want to stop by and see for yourself. If you do, please remember to be respectful. Cemeteries are meant to be peaceful final resting places. Your presence there should never disturb anyone, living or dead.

Strange Sights
at Snuffer's

When most people think of Snuffer's Restaurant, the first thing that comes to mind is the delicious cheddar fries. Just the thought of those hot, crispy fries topped with melted cheddar cheese, bacon, and chives will make your stomach growl. But the original Snuffer's location in Lower Greenville is also famous for something else—its ghosts!

According to the waitstaff at Snuffer's, strange things happen after hours when they are closing up. Lights will swing back and forth when nothing is there to move them, and glasses have been known to move several feet while a waiter's back is turned. Some have seen a woman in black drifting through the restaurant, and one staff member was shocked to see the ghostly figure of a woman sitting atop the vending machine one night.

Snuffer's first opened its doors at 3526 Greenville Avenue in 1978. Before becoming a restaurant that delighted customers with burgers and fries, the building housed a pool hall that sometimes catered to a rowdy crowd. Some think this may explain the source of the Snuffer's ghosts.

Even after major renovations and an addition to the original structure, spirits continued to show up. One L-shaped hallway in the back room was a particularly popular area for supernatural sightings. A featureless, dark, shadowy figure frequently appeared in the small corridor, moving from the new addition to the original structure. Each time, the ghost disappeared when it arrived at the main building. The image of this shadowy specter gave a fright to all who witnessed it, but the apparition never interacted with the living. It seemed unaware of anyone around and simply continued its ghostly passage through the hall.

In 2013, the original Snuffer's building was demolished and rebuilt, but even that did not keep customers from the other side away. Strange things still occur at Snuffer's on Greenville. Maybe it's the wonderful aroma of cheddar fries that keeps the ghosts coming back.

The Lady of White Rock Lake

Picture this: You've spent the day at Dallas's lovely White Rock Lake. You hiked the nature trails, kayaked on the beautiful blue water, and had a picnic in the park amid the trees and wildflowers. As the sun begins to set, coloring the sky a brilliant orange, you understand why this space is called the "jewel in the crown" of the Dallas Park System.

Night has fallen when you leave the lake. You are driving down a dark street when your car's headlights flash upon an unexpected sight. A young woman stands on the side of the road. She's dressed in a white evening gown, and her long hair is sopping wet even though it's not raining. On the one hand, it's dangerous to pick up a hitchhiker. On the other hand, this girl is obviously in distress.

You pull over. The young woman asks for a ride. She says she was in an accident and ended up in the lake. She wants to be dropped off at a house on Gaston Avenue, a few blocks away. You agree to drive her there, and she climbs into the back seat.

On the way to the address, you turn around to ask the woman a question . . . but she's gone. The back seat is empty except for a wet stain where the young hitchhiker was sitting.

This spine-shivering scenario has been happening to drivers passing by White Rock Lake for years. They see a young lady in a drenched white dress standing on the side of the road by the lake. They give her a ride only to have her vanish on the way to her destination.

Long ago, an even eerier version of this ghostly sighting occurred. As the legend goes, one kind-hearted driver who picked up the ghostly girl drove her all the way to the address she gave, but when they arrived, she had fallen asleep in the car. Not wanting to wake her, the driver knocked on the door of the house. When a couple answered the door, the driver explained that their daughter had been in an accident, but she was okay and asleep in the backseat of the car. At this news, the couple became upset. The father, angered by the cruel joke, replied that their daughter had died in an accident years ago, and he slammed the door. Confused, the driver went back to his car only to find the girl gone, the backseat wet where she had been sleeping.

White Rock Lake was constructed in 1910. Its purpose was to supply water to Dallas, but the city also wanted it to be a pretty space where residents could enjoy the outdoors. They certainly achieved this goal. Today, the lake and surrounding park appeal to joggers, bikers, and families with their natural beauty and opportunities for recreation. But when night falls, the area's charm is tinged with a heavy layer of spookiness.

Who is the Lady of White Rock Lake? Some people believe the spirit is the ghost of Hallie Gaston, a 19-year-old woman who drowned in

the lake on May 27, 1927, when the boat she and her friends were on capsized. This story makes a lot of sense (even though Gaston Avenue was named after Confederate soldier William Henry Gaston, not Hallie). Then again, other people say the ghost in the white dress was the daughter of a wealthy Dallas family on her way home from a party when her car crashed into the lake.

Whoever the Lady of White Rock Lake is, she likes making appearances, and not just to cars. People on the docks late in the evening have also glimpsed her ghostly form slowly

floating toward them. In 1987, a woman and her daughter were sitting on the dock, enjoying a peaceful evening at the lake when they saw an apparition in the water. Closer and closer the figure floated, until finally the pair realized with terror that they were looking at the corpse of a woman! However, as soon as they understood what they were seeing, the image disappeared.

A Dallas police officer once spotted the ghost, too. He saw a sopping wet woman walking out of the reeds by the lake, but when he went to check on her, she vanished.

Perhaps the creepiest thing about the Lady of White Rock Lake is that she doesn't always stay at the lake. Homeowners near the area have reported seeing her as well. One man says his doorbell rang over and over one night. Each time he answered, no one was there. Then, finally, he opened the door to see the familiar sight of the lady in white standing on his doorstep. She disappeared immediately.

There's also a haunted bridge by the lake. People say if you stop your car on the bridge on Lawther Drive, the engine will die. Is the Lady of the Lake trying to warn drivers not to lose control of their cars and end up like her? Or is her motive more sinister than that? Is she,

instead, trying to lure some company into the water's depths?

And what about the hauntings at nearby Flag Pole Hill Park? Just north of White Rock Lake is another popular recreational area for Dallasites. Flag Pole Hill Park offers scenic views, walking trails, picnic areas, and great playgrounds where kids and adults can have a good time on a sunny day. But it also comes

with its share of unexplained phenomena. People have seen flickering lights at the top of the hill with no known source, and people driving past the north end of the park have reported rocks flying toward their cars from strange angles. Is the Lady of White Rock Lake responsible for those strange occurrences, too? Or is something else to blame for the eerie encounters? Everything from UFOs to Satan worshippers has been suggested to explain the events.

There's no way to know for sure who, or what, or how many entities are haunting the area around White Rock Lake. What we *do* know is that the lake is a beautiful spot to spend some time in the daylight ... and maybe somewhere you don't want to linger after dark.

CHAPTER 6

Unexpected Experiences at Unity of Dallas

What would it take to get you to move somewhere you didn't want to live? For the wife of R.B. Evans, Jr., it took a very specific house.

When R.B. Evans, Jr. moved to Texas in the 1940s, his wife didn't want to go with him. She told him she would only leave Mississippi if he built her a house that looked just like the one he'd grown up in. Mrs. Evans probably thought her husband would not follow through on this request, and she would never have to leave her home. However, R.B. did as she asked and built her a two-story Greek Revival Colonial-style house on what is now Forest Lane in Dallas. It was a grand structure that looked like something out of the movie *Gone with the Wind*. Her husband had fulfilled his promise, so Mrs. Evans lived up to her part of the bargain and moved to Texas with him.

Today, the Evans home is the site of a church called Unity of Dallas, but some odd phenomena in the building suggest that the house's original owners may still be around. Guests at weddings and other events at Unity have heard piano music coming from the second floor where no piano is located. Others have heard conversations, but when they go to see who's chatting, they find no one there. Doors will mysteriously open themselves at Unity, and random cold spots appear where none should be. A few people there have actually seen a ghost. The apparition is of a woman in white who stands upstairs or floats, *glowing,* through the building's empty rooms.

Even though Mrs. Evans never wanted to move to Texas, it's possible she loved her new Dallas home more than she thought she would. Maybe she loved it so much, in fact, that her spirit never left.

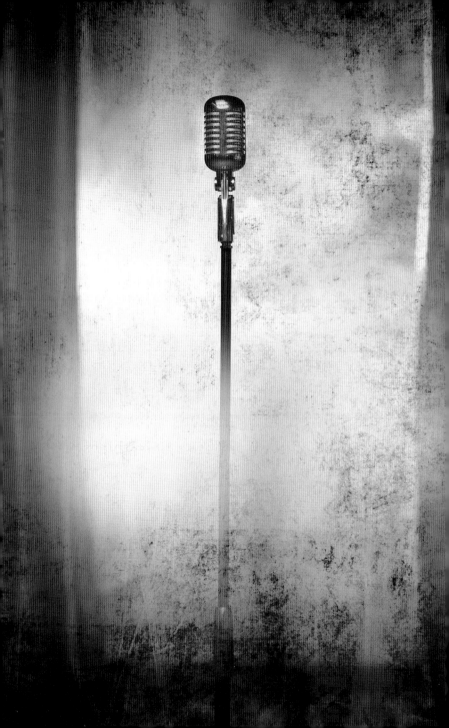

Ghosts with Good Taste

Art, music, beautiful gardens—most people believe these are some of the finer things in life. As it turns out, Dallas's ghosts agree. They enjoy experiencing the city's cultural side just as much as its living residents.

The beauty of the Dallas Arboretum on Garland Road will take your breath away. The sixty-six-acre botanical gardens on the shore of White Rock Lake delight visitors with local flora, sculptures, and holiday festivities while also educating them about horticulture (the care of gardens and plants).

The centerpiece of the Arboretum is the DeGolyer House, a 21,000-square-foot home built in the 1940s for Everette DeGolyer and his wife. Everette was a successful oil executive as well as a philanthropist, which means he was very generous with his good fortune. After the DeGolyers both passed away, the house was donated to SMU (Southern Methodist University), who later gave it to the City of Dallas. The estate is enormous, consisting of thirteen rooms, seven bathrooms, five fireplaces, and seven chimneys. The library alone is 1,750 square feet, which is larger than many ordinary homes in the Dallas area. It is this huge, historic house that is rumored to be haunted. Although many oppose the rumors, saying there are no ghosts at the Arboretum, some employees have experienced strange situations and claim something supernatural is *definitely* happening there.

One guide described a particularly unsettling event that happened to her at the DeGolyer House.

She was leaving the house one night when she realized she'd left her keys inside. However, when she returned for them, they were not where she'd put them down. As she searched for the keys, she heard odd noises coming from somewhere else in the house and decided to investigate. When she opened the door to the living room, a cold chill enveloped her. She turned on the light and saw that things were out of order. The lid of the piano was open, though it always remained closed, and a photo of Mr. DeGolyer was not where it should have been. Feeling the need to put things back as they belonged, the guide stepped forward. Then, all of a sudden, shivers crawled up her spine, and she got a creepy feeling that she shouldn't touch anything in the room. She hurried out, quickly found her keys, and left as fast as she could.

The following morning, she was the first to arrive at the DeGolyer House. When she entered the living room, the piano was closed, and Mr. DeGolyer's photo was back where it belonged.

For spirits more interested in guitars than gardens, the Sons of Hermann Hall is the place to be. The Sons of Hermann Hall—the oldest free-standing wood structure in Dallas—is a fraternal society, which is a club of people, usually men, who devote their time to social, professional, or charitable activities. The original Sons of Hermann society was founded in 1840 by German immigrants in New York, but the organization grew and expanded until it eventually made its way to Texas in 1860. By 1911, there were four lodges in the Dallas area. That's when they combined into one larger group and built the structure that still stands at 3414 Elm Street today.

The part of Elm Street where the Hall is located is known as Deep Elum, an entertainment district considered to be the live music capital of North Texas. Sons of Hermann Hall is a popular venue for concerts and dancing, and it has had more than a few brushes with fame over the years. The long-running TV show *Dallas* once filmed an episode there, and in 1986, the upstairs ballroom was leased for six months to be the police headquarters in the sci-fi movie *Robocop*. Then, in 2002, Kelly Clarkson, the first-ever "American Idol," passed her first audition at the Hall.

However, some the most interesting characters in the building are the anonymous ones. No one knows exactly who is haunting the Sons of Hermann Hall, but it's clear that something spooky is going on there.

Lights go on and off on their own at the Hall, and doors open and close for no reason, sometimes even locking themselves. Often, employees clean up at night and leave, only to return the next day to find things out of order. Either objects are moving around on their own during the night, or some jokester spirit is playing tricks on the people who work there. It's possible these creepy comedians are children because childish voices have been heard on the staircase. However, at least one of the ghosts is an adult because people have seen an unknown man walking around inside the building, but when they try to follow him, he disappears.

The ghosts of Sons of Hermann Hall seem perfectly content with the music venue they've chosen to haunt, but souls from the other side who want something a little different may be drawn to the Sammons Center for the Arts, just a few miles away on Harry Hines Boulevard. The Sammons Center for the Arts provides a space for nonprofit performing arts organizations to meet, rehearse, and perform. The Center is known for its jazz concerts and cabaret shows and for the members' strong support of the arts community.

The building where the Sammons Center for the Arts makes its home used to be the Turtle Creek Pump Station. A pump station, or pumphouse, is a storage chamber that lifts wastewater and sewage when gravity alone can't move it where it needs to go. This may not sound like a very glamorous use for a building, but this pumphouse was actually a beautiful structure: red brick with arched windows and interesting architectural details. It was designed by the architectural firm C.S. Gill & Sons, a company that also designed Dallas's third city hall and many of the city's most striking homes.

The Turtle Creek Pump Station was built in 1909 and served as the water source for the entire city of Dallas until 1930. After that, the building went through changes and remodeling for other uses and then was eventually left abandoned until it looked like a haunted house out of a movie with its broken windows, rust, and sagging ceilings. Thankfully, the Dallas City Council declared the historic building a landmark in 1981. Renovations restored it to its original grandeur, and the building started its new life as the Sammons Center for the Arts.

When the old pump station was brought back to life, no one was as happy about its resurrection as the ghost who calls the building home. The spirit's name is unknown, but whoever he is, he seems to be having a good time. Witnesses say the ghost is a man wearing overalls and a worker's cap, and some have begun calling him "Otis" because he loves to play with the building's elevator, which was made by the famous Otis Elevator Company. "Otis" likes to move the elevator up and down on its own, even when no one has called it. Sometimes, when employees arrive for work in the morning, the elevator opens its doors for them before they've even pushed the button. What a polite ghost! Skeptics who don't believe in the supernatural say it's just a mechanical problem, but the Center's service

crews say they have replaced almost every part, and the elevator keeps acting like it has a mind of its own.

"Otis" especially enjoys playing jokes on women. He steals items from the female employees' desks and returns them again a few days later. Why? Who knows! Maybe it's his attempt at flirting. Whatever his reasons, the ghost seems to be enjoying himself. People sometimes hear singing and laughter when no one else is around.

Though "Otis's" real identity is unknown, some believe he may have been a young worker who died in an accident in the basement when the building was still a pumphouse. People used to report cold spots and a feeling of being watched down there. Also, it is interesting to note that when the pump station was remodeled in the 1980s, the basement was left alone. Only the elevator shaft was utilized in the new building.

If you're looking for culture in Dallas, check out the picturesque botanical gardens of the Arboretum, listen to some live music in Deep Elum, or enjoy a show at the Sammons Center for the Arts. You'll be in good company with the best of Dallas's present—*and* past.

Spooky Suburbs

After eating at Snuffer's, walking around White Rock Lake, visiting Old City Park, and paying your respects at the Sixth Floor Museum, you may be feeling a little spooked. Your nerves may be on edge, and the hairs on the back of your neck may need some convincing to lie back down again. Perhaps you need a break from encounters with the otherworldly. Well, escaping Dallas's ghosts isn't so easy because the towns surrounding Dallas are haunted, too!

If you've seen all the creepy characters Dallas has to offer and you're still craving more eerie experiences, these spooky suburbs are just a short drive away.

RED OAK

Warning! This ghostly tale includes some gruesome details. Read with care.

Twenty miles south of Dallas in Red Oak, Texas, the Reindeer Manor Haunted House has been offering scares to thrill-seekers for years. Every October, customers enjoy screaming their way through Reindeer Manor's many terrifying attractions for a price. However, the property where the current business creates fake horror has its own very chilling—and very *real*—haunted history.

In the early 1900s, a man named James Sharp owned a two-story house on the land where Reindeer Manor now sits. He rented the home to a Swedish immigrant family. In 1915, during a violent thunderstorm, lightning struck the wooden house, setting it on fire. The entire family was killed in the blaze.

Sharp rebuilt the house, this time using stronger, more fireproof materials. His plan was to make it a grand home for his own family to live in. However, his dream did not come true. During construction, while his wife and children were still living in New York waiting for the house to be completed, Sharp died of a gunshot wound. But how he was shot is unclear. Some say he shot himself, while others claim he was murdered.

Construction on the house continued after Sharp's death, and in 1920, his oldest son, Matt, moved in. Matt enjoyed success in farming, ranching, and breeding horses for several years. He did so well that he was able to add a carriage house and servants' quarters to the property. However, in 1929 during the Great Depression, the Sharp family lost all their money.

Matt's wife was a spiritualist, and she believed their family's home was cursed. Together, they held séances, sought advice from psychics and witch doctors, mixed potions, and chanted incantations in the hopes of ridding their house of the bad luck they believed followed them. However, their attempts to break the curse were unsuccessful, and Matt and his wife also met a tragic end. She died by poisoning in the dining room of the house, and Matt was found hanging from a noose in the barn. After that, the manor fell into ruin. It remained empty until 1974 when the owners of Reindeer Manor Haunted House took over.

With such a sad and violent history, it's no wonder that a few real hauntings have been reported at Reindeer Manor. Employees working there during the Halloween season often hear strange sounds, such as voices or a woman's moans. People run into unexplained cold spots, and sometimes feel a person brush up against them when no one is there. In the barn, where Matt's body was found, workers have seen an unexplainable dark shadow moving around. And lights sometimes dance through the windows of the buildings even when the property is closed.

Is there still a curse on the site of Reindeer Manor? No one knows for sure. But if you visit during the Halloween season for a scare, just remember that some of the ghosts might be real.

WAXAHACHIE

A few miles down the road from Red Oak, the town of Waxahachie waits with its own spine-tingling stories to tell. Waxahachie was founded in 1850, and many of the beautiful Victorian homes from the late 1800s remain, earning the town the nickname "Gingerbread City." The Gingerbread Home Tour takes guests to some of the ornate old houses, but there are a few other stops you might want to check out if you're looking for the spookier side of the suburb.

A couple of Waxahachie's most haunted locations have recently closed their doors, but that doesn't mean the ghosts are gone. They may still be lingering in the area looking for someplace new to haunt.

One of the Gingerbread City's haunted addresses was 414 W. Main Street. This old Victorian mansion used to be the Bonny Nook Inn, which gave the feeling of being crowded even when it wasn't full of guests. The house was once the home of a doctor, his wife, and his wife's sister. In the early 1900s, an explosion in the kitchen killed the doctor's wife. A few months later,

Victorian House in Waxahachie

he married her sister, which some thought was a bit scandalous. In 1980, when new owners bought the house to renovate it for a bed-and-breakfast, they were told there was a room on the second floor that had not been unlocked since 1910. Undeterred by superstitions, the owners opened it. Some say maybe they shouldn't have. That room became the epicenter of strange occurrences at the Bonny Nook Inn. Shadows, voices, and the sounds of lullabies sung in a foreign language plagued the space. Whether it was the doctor's wife's spirit haunting the house or someone else, no one knows for sure.

Another haunted Waxahachie structure that has since gone out of business was the Catfish Plantation at 814 Water Street. The Cajun-style restaurant was located in another Victorian house dating back to 1895. Not long after Tom and Melissa Baker opened the

Catfish Plantation in 1984, odd things began happening. Tea urns relocated from their place on the counter to the middle of the floor during the night, and sometimes the owners arrived to open the restaurant in the morning to find fresh-brewed coffee already waiting for them. Now, that's the kind of ghost I'd like to have! Employees also reported baskets floating through the air, glowing lights coming from rooms no one was in, and silverware or trays shaking without being touched by human hands.

When paranormal investigators visited the Catfish Plantation, they found several spirits hanging out there, including a man who liked to flirt with the young female employees, a woman named Caroline who owned the house in a previous decade, and a man named Will who died in the house in the 1930s. Will enjoyed spending time on the porch where he was sometimes seen by customers waiting for a table. The most distraught ghost in the restaurant was named Elizabeth. This poor woman had been strangled to death by an ex-boyfriend in the house on her wedding day. Employees sometimes glimpsed the image of a woman in a wedding dress standing in one of the windows, felt cold spots in that area of the building, or caught the scent of roses in the air.

The Catfish Plantation is closed now, but that doesn't mean Caroline and Will and Elizabeth are gone. (So whoever inhabits the house at 814 Water Street today should be on the lookout for them!)

One ghostly place still open to guests is the Rogers Hotel at 100 College Street in downtown Waxahachie. After Emory W. Rogers's first two hotels burned down in the late 1800s and early 1900s, he built the current structure of reinforced concrete, making it as fireproof as possible. Construction was completed in 1913, and the building has stood ever since. The hotel was designed with some unique features, including a panoramic view of the city from the top of one tower and an open-air space on the top of the other tower where guests could sleep in tents under the stars. The basement was equipped with a barbershop, billiard room, and swimming pool filled with warm water from a nearby hot springs.

The Rogers Hotel *also* happens to be overflowing with tales of supernatural experiences. From voices heard in room 409, to elevators moving on their own, to faucets turning on and off when no one is in the bathroom, it seems like everyone who spends a night there has a story to tell. One man was sitting on the bed putting on his shoes when he felt a cold breeze and then pressure on the mattress, as if someone had just sat down next to him. A woman once woke up to see a cowboy standing over her bed. While she was staring at him, he disappeared!

The most unsettling sensations occur in the basement of the

building. The space gives off a creepy feeling, and photos taken there reveal mysterious balls of light. A handyman named Melvin was working in the hotel when a ghost approached him and beckoned him to follow. Melvin did. The ghost led him to the boiler room in the basement and told him to stay away from that place because it was evil and people had died there. Melvin ran back to his room and installed extra locks on his door. Maybe after that, he thought twice before following a ghost.

CLEBURNE

About an hour southwest of Dallas, the town of Cleburne is a great place to visit if you like shopping for antiques, going to museums, or enjoying nature. It's also a good destination for ghost hunters. Cleburne's ghosts all like to hang out at the same place—the Wright Plaza.

The Wright Building, which takes up a fourth of a city block between Main Street and Caddo, was built in 1893 and added onto in 1916. The two-story, red brick structure has housed numerous businesses in its time, including hotels, toy stores, shoe stores, restaurants, and even a haunted house attraction for a while. Companies come and go in the building, but the spirits have stuck around.

Wright Plaza has several characters haunting its halls. One is the ghost of a young woman named Lillie who was pushed out of a window to her death when the building was the Hamilton House Hotel. Poor Lillie came to Cleburne in 1882, the only survivor in her whole family after the Civil War. She was just twenty-seven when she died. Witnesses have seen Lillie's figure hovering in the very window where she breathed her last breath.

Lillie may have been alone when she arrived at Wright Plaza, but she has plenty of company now. Ghost hunters have detected at least four more ghosts on the second floor, including a hunchbacked woman, a German cobbler (a person who mends shoes), and the cobbler's wife and niece. With so many spirits hanging around up there, it's no surprise people have experienced some strange sensations in the

building. Visitors claim to smell oranges and cigar smoke that cannot be explained, and sometimes they feel someone lightly touch them when no human is nearby. Otherworldly sounds also haunt the second floor, such as the laughter of children and the tapping of nails . . . *just* like the sound a cobbler would make as he mends a pair of shoes.

Mysteries in McKinney

What would you do if you were visiting a historic home and saw a little girl in a white dress standing at the top of the stairs? How would you feel if you found out the store employee who'd just helped you find the item you were looking for was actually a *ghost?* How would you react if you were eating a slice of pie at a café when you saw a shadow man walk by? What would you do if I told you there was a place you could go to experience all these things?

Thirty miles north of Dallas is a suburb that deserves its own spotlight. McKinney's ghostly activity is definitely worth the trip.

Originally called The Peters Colony, the area was first settled in 1841. In 1848, the town was named McKinney, and it became the county seat of Collin County. Both were named after Collin McKinney, a pioneer who helped draft the Texas Declaration of Independence from Mexico in 1936.

McKinney began to develop, opening businesses and welcoming new residents. But after the Houston and Texas Central Railroad came through in 1872, the town really grew, becoming a major source of cotton and crops such as corn, wheat, and oats. In 1875, McKinney's first official courthouse was completed and, for a time, it was the tallest building north of San Antonio. Today, the new courthouse is a few miles away on Bloomdale Road, but the Old Collin County Courthouse still sits on Chestnut Square in downtown McKinney, a bustling area popular for its shopping, dining, holiday festivities, and spooky sightings. McKinney's ghosts are so popular, the town hosts an annual Ghost Walk in October that offers participants a chance to tour some of their favorite haunts. There was even a group of ghost hunters from TEXPART Paranormal who used to frequently visit McKinney to conduct supernatural research!

So, where do McKinney's ghosts like to hang out? The better question might be where *don't* they like to hang out! The Chestnut Square Historic Village, the Performing Arts Center, the Old Collin County Prison,

The Pantry, and Landon Winery are only some of the places where people have experienced eerie phenomena over the years.

The Chestnut Square Historic Village just south of downtown McKinney is dedicated to preserving history and educating the community about the past. The village consists of ten structures dating from 1854 to 1930, and a couple of them are haunted. The Dulaney House is a beautiful prairie-style home at the corner of Chestnut and Anthony Street. The two-story yellow house with white trim was built in 1916 by John Field, who constructed the home for his sister, Lucy Field Dulaney. Lucy's husband had passed away, leaving her to raise their children alone. Today, visitors sometimes hear slamming doors or footsteps

upstairs at the Dulaney House when no one is walking there. Some have also seen the image of a little girl in a white dress standing near the attic door. This could be the ghost of Mrs. Dulaney's daughter, who died of an illness when she was just a child.

Ghostly happenings also occur at the Two-Bit Taylor Inn. This old two-story building once served as a bed-and-breakfast where travelers could spend a night in the attic room for just "two bits," which was slang for twenty-five cents. The tale of the Two-Bit Taylor Inn says you can sometimes see a man dressed in a Civil War uniform looking out of the attic window.

The McKinney hauntings continue a few blocks away at the Old Collin County Prison on South Kentucky Street, and the tale people tell about that building is sure to send shivers up your spine. The structure hasn't been used as a jail since 1979, but before that, it served as a prison for decades, and in the early 1900s, the county even held executions there. In 1922, Ezell Stepp was the last man sentenced to death at the Collin County Prison. He was convicted of murder and executed by hanging. Rumor has it, Stepp's death left a lasting impression. People say, when the light is just right, you can still see the shadow of the hanged man in the courtyard.

Across the street from the Old Collin County Prison sits the McKinney Performing Arts Center, which makes its residence in the former courthouse building. The structure at 111 North Tennessee Street served as the Collin County Courthouse from 1876 to 1979. Today, patrons visit to see comedies, concerts, plays, and musicals, but even before it was a performing arts center, the building had its own share of drama. Legend says a heartbroken woman took her own life in the courthouse after her husband filed for divorce there. Ever since, the image of a woman in white can sometimes be seen peering out a top-floor window.

In addition to the unfortunate events that took place inside the old courthouse's walls, employees there had a front-row seat to one of McKinney's biggest tragedies. On January 23, 1913, a three-story building across the street from the courthouse collapsed. The building was home to the T.J. Tingle Implement Store and the Cheeves Brothers & Co. Dry Goods Store (also known as the Mississippi Store). Cheeves Brothers had been holding a sale that day, so the crowd of shoppers was larger than usual. When the walls and ceilings crumbled, people in the neighboring buildings watched in helpless horror as dozens were trapped beneath the debris. Ten people died in the department store disaster, and many more suffered injuries. It's likely that some of McKinney's ghosts surfaced from this tragedy.

Less than two hundred feet from the Performing Arts Center, the Landon Winery on Kentucky Street has a problem keeping stock on the shelves, and it's not just because people love to shop there. In fact, bottles of wine used to fly off the highest shelves for no reason! This happened so often, employees began leaving the top shelves empty. Doors also open and close on their own. No one knows who the spirits are, but the winery does have one unique feature that could shed some light on the strange activity.

When the Landon Winery was under construction, the builders discovered an eighteen-foot-deep well dating back to the mid-1800s. Rather than filling it in, they chose to maintain the history of the land and simply built around the well. Perhaps the ghostly hands that topple wine bottles and play with doors climbed up from beneath the ground? After all, in folklore, fairies have been known to gather at wells.

A couple of blocks away, The Pantry, a popular restaurant serving homestyle cooking, also has trouble keeping things where they're supposed to be. Pans fall off shelves without being touched, and the smell of fire sometimes drifts through from an unseen source. If that's not creepy enough, customers and employees have seen a "shadow man" wandering around. The building where the restaurant serves delicious pies and comfort food has been around for over a hundred years, so the ghosts haunting the location could have been there a *long* time.

Other McKinney businesses that have closed their doors in recent years also used to house spirits. For instance, Buffalo Joe's, formerly of Tennessee Street, had a playful ghost in its storage room. The spirit used to unroll brand-new rolls of toilet paper and stick forks into the wall. What a prankster! And at Morningstar Treasures, once on Louisiana Street, a very helpful young man used to assist customers with finding the items they needed. The problem was, he didn't work at the store, and perhaps . . . was not even alive.

The building that housed Morningstar was constructed in 1888 and was originally home to the J.P. Dowell Hardware Store. The shop sold such high-quality goods that it earned an excellent reputation and was nicknamed the "Neiman Marcus of McKinney," after the luxury department store. In the building's days as Morningstar Treasures, apparitions dressed in Victorian clothing were spotted more than once, sometimes dressed in mourning attire, as if they were grieving the loss of a loved one. Some believe the helpful young man was actually the ghost of a former employee who died young in 1925, described in his obituary as a "trusted, faithful, and untiring employee" of the J.P. Dowell Hardware Store.

Just because Buffalo Joe's and Morningstar Treasures aren't around anymore doesn't mean their ghosts are gone, too. Spirits that

have already stuck around a century aren't very likely to pack up and move just because a business closes its doors, so the current occupants of 100 N. Tennessee Street and 208 E. Louisiana Street should keep an eye out. But even if those ghosts have moved on, it's clear McKinney still has a lot to offer to anyone seeking signs of the supernatural.

A Ghostly Goodbye

Dallas has a lot to offer residents, tourists, and those searching for some spooky scenery. After strolling the trails at the Arboretum, shopping downtown, visiting museums, and spending the night at a fancy hotel, it can be hard to leave the city lovingly nicknamed the Big D.

But don't worry.

Like the many ghosts who inhabit the city, you can always come back. You won't find a kinder place to haunt than Dallas.

Carie Juettner was born on Halloween and has loved ghost stories ever since. When she's not writing books, she loves to read, do yoga, and take long walks in the woods. Carie lives in Richardson, Texas, with her husband and pets, but she loves to travel. One of her favorite things to do on vacation is visit cemeteries and learn about local lore. To find out more about Carie, visit her website: cariejuettner.com.

Check out some of the other *Spooky America* titles available now!

Spooky America was adapted from the creeptastic *Haunted America* series for adults. *Haunted America* explores historical haunts in cities and regions across America. Here's more from the original *Haunted Dallas* author Rita Cook: